Let's Talk About
BEING BOSSY

Let's Talk About
BEING BOSSY

By JOY BERRY

Illustrated by John Costanza
Edited by Kate Dickey
Designed by Abigail Johnston

GROLIER ENTERPRISES CORP.

Let's talk about BEING BOSSY.

Bossy people want to have their way all of the time.

Bossy people think they know what is best for everyone. They think they know what everyone should and should not do.

Bossy people tell others what to do and expect them to do what they are told to do.

Bossy people expect others to obey them.

Some bossy people try to *bribe others* into obeying.

They promise to give something to the people who obey them.

Some bossy people try to *threaten others* into obeying.

They say that they will go away or not play with the people who will not obey them.

Some bossy people try to *frighten others* into obeying.

They act as though they will hurt the people who will not obey them.

Most people want to have their own way some of the time.

They do not want others always telling them what to do. They do not like to be bossed.

If you are like most people, you do not want
to be bossed.

It is important to treat other people
the way you want to be treated.

If you do not like being bossed, you should not
be bossy.

Try not to be bossy.

Realize that you cannot have your way
all of the time. It is not good for you.
It is not fair to the people around you.

Take turns deciding who will choose
what to do when you are with other people.
If you choose one activity, let the other people
choose the next activity.

Make sure you suggest an acceptable activity when it is your turn to choose.

- Choose an activity that is safe.

- Be sure your parents and other people's parents approve the activity.

- Choose something that everyone will enjoy.

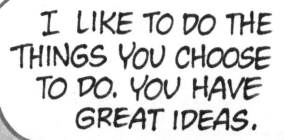

Be a good sport when it is the other people's turn to choose an activity.

- Do whatever they choose to do if it is safe and if your parents and the other people's parents approve.

- Try not to complain.

- Do whatever you can to make the activity enjoyable for everyone.

Try not to be bossy. Do not bribe, threaten, or frighten anyone into obeying you.

No one likes to be bossed. If you do not want
to be bossed, you must not be bossy.